EXCEL
VBA

Programming For Complete Beginners, Step-By-Step Illustrated Guide to Mastering Excel VBA

Complementary Book

SQL: Programming for Complete Beginners

CONTENTS

Introduction

Getting Started!

Hello, *there future Excel Programmers!* Thanks for viewing this book. This book has been designed to be your go-to book for excel programming. It is drafted in simple English to make your programming experience fun and easy. It's fine even if you don't have the slightest idea about Excel VBA, this book will help you get a grab on the programming in no time. (With just a *little* effort) Before going further, I would like to tell my prospective readers that who exactly is the target audience for this book. Please find below my assumption about you:

- ✓ You do have an access to a computer (A laptop or a desktop). The computers, in turn, have a connection to the internet.
- ✓ You are a frequent user of the Microsoft Excel tool

What is Excel VBA?

I am sure you must be excited to jump into the bandwagon of the Excel Programmers. Well, hold your horses a little for now, as this chapter will first give you some critical background information that will help you become an fantastic Excel Programmer.The term VBA stands for *Visual Basic* for *Applications*. This programming language was developed by Microsoft Company. VBA is the tool that is going to help us control and customize the functionalities of the Excel. Throughout this book, you will get to see the term *"Macros"* a lot as well. Before you confuse yourself, let me explain what macros is. The codes that are written to perform operations in excel is known as Macros. VBA, however, is the programming language platform where Macros are written. This is how VBA and

Macros are interlinked. The VBA tool can be convenient to perform thousands of different tasks. Here are a few scenarios:

- ✓ It can help in analyzing data
- ✓ It can help us in forecasting and budgeting of data
- ✓ Automating our reports to save up time and improve efficiency
- ✓ Conveying data into visuals such as charts, graphs etc

them, the Word doc should look like the PDF file. I can go on and on with the tasks it can perform, but hopefully, you do now have an idea about its functionalities. In a nutshell, VBA tool helps to speed up the operations performed on excel. Let's take an example, every day you get an excel sheet containing a list of employees with some necessary information. You have to manually perform some formatting like to make the name bold, make the phone number right aligned, and add some colors to the rows. Now if the list of employees is long so doing it manually every day can be an extremely tedious task. This is basically where the VBA tool comes in handy. You can write a macro code regarding all the formatting steps, place a button on your sheet and finally bind the macros with the button. Just one hit and you're good to go.

* * *

Jumping into the VBA Tool

Before we jump deep into the swimming pool, learning to swim should be our topmost agenda. This section is going to give you a feel of the entire VBA tool. It will give you a good grab on the basics.

To get started on the VBA tool, we first need to access the most crucial tab: Developer. Follow the steps to access the tab:

1. Open the Excel tool
2. Right Click on any area of the Ribbon and then select the customize option

3. Once the customize tab is open, you can find the developer option in the second column
4. Check the Developer Option
5. Click Ok

Congratulations! You now have a brand-new tab on your Excel tool: Developer. By clicking on the developer tab, we will be navigated to the section that is of interest to all the VBA programmers. We will now be performing our very first exercise on the VBA tool. The macro that we are going to write will perform the following functions:

✓ Type name into a cell
✓ Enter the current date and time into a cell
✓ Bold the text entered in the name cell
✓ Change the font size of the date cell to 14

* * *

Recording the Macros

In this section, we will be performing an exercise to learn how to record the Macros. Excel has a built-in functionality in which the user doesn't have to manually write the code. The tool has the option to record all the operations that you are performing and then finally generate a macro code for it.The macro we will write now won't win us the first prize in a VBA programming competition but to reach your final destination one needs to take baby steps. Following are the steps that we will follow to write our very first code.

1. Open the Excel Tool
2. Click on the developer tab
3. Select a cell on the excel worksheet. Click on any cell
4. On the developers' tab, click on the Record Macro Button
5. As shown below, the Record Macros box is displayed
6. Now we will be entering a name for the Macros. The default name is Macro 1 but its always advisable to give a better name

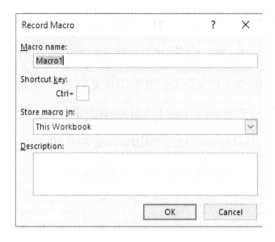

1. Click in the shortcut key and enter a shortcut key. For now, we will be entering shift+N so our shortcut key will be ctrl+shift+N

2. On macro dialogue box, the option that says "store in:" should be set to "This Workbook"

3. Click Ok. The macros will now start to record.

4. Type your name on the cell where you want to display it

5. Now in the adjacent cell, enter the below formula

   `=Now()`

6. Now we will convert the formula to its value. For this right click on the date cell, select copy. Now

right-click on the cell again, and select paste values(V).

7. Now Select the cell where you entered your name. Go to the home tab, traverse to the font section and select bold(B). Also, change the font size to 14.

8. Now to stop recording, go to the developer section. Select stop recording.

Cheers! Your first project for the Excel VBA macro is finished.

To ensure that your macros are working fine, you should test your code. Move the cursor to an empty cell, press Ctrl+Shift+N. Within a snap, the excel code will be executed. Your name, date and time will be displayed on the sheet. You can also view the code that has been recorded by the excel tool. Go to the developer tab, and click on macros. You can now view the code that was automatically generated

behind the operations that you just performed. Below is the code that was generated.

```vba
Sub MyName()
'
' MyName Macro
'

    Range("B2").Select
    ActiveCell.FormulaR1C1 = "Anum"
    Range("C2").Select
    ActiveCell.FormulaR1C1 = "=NOW()"
    Range("B2").Select
    Selection.Font.Bold = True
    With Selection.Font
        .Name = "Calibri"
        .Size = 14
        .Strikethrough = False
        .Superscript = False
        .Subscript = False
        .OutlineFont = False
        .Shadow = False
        .Underline = xlUnderlineStyleNone
        .ThemeColor = xlThemeColorLight1
        .TintAndShade = 0
        .ThemeFont = xlThemeFontMinor
    End With
End Sub
```

The first statement recognizes as the sub procedure and gives the name of the macro that you entered. The second statement identifies that cell "B2" is selected. B2 means a second column and second row on the excel sheet. The third statement then highlights the name you entered on Cell B2. Cell b3 is then selected and then the Now() formula was entered. Selection.font.bold= true indicates that the cell formatting was changed to bold. The sub-procedure finally ends the code by the End sub Procedure.

Chapter 1: VBA Variables

Value holders

Let me introduce you to real programming language element called variable. Just like other programming languages, VBA has elements common to them. The main agenda of the VBA tool is to manipulate data. VBA can store the data to the computer's memory. Some of the data that you create is stored in variables. A named storage location in the computer's memory is known as a variable. Excel gives us the flexibility to name the variables whatever we want them to be. To assign a value to the variable, we use the equal sign operator. Let's look at some of the examples of the variables.

```
a = 1
PerformanceRate = 0.95
EmployeeSalary = 123455
DataEntered = False
a = a + 1
UserName = "Anum Haroon"
```

There are specific rules when declaring variables in the VBA tool:

✓ The first letter of the variable should be a character.   The rest can be numbers, letters, or punctuation characters

✓ There is no distinguishment between the upper-case and lower-case letters when declaring variables

✓ A variable name should be without any space

✓ Special characters such #, $, %, &, or! cannot be used in the variable name

✓ The size of the variable name should not exceed 255 characters

To better understand the variables, most programmers use mix cases, for example, PerformanceRate or Employee_Salary.

The VBA tool also puts some restriction on the variable names. Words such as Dim, End, With, Sub, Next and For cannot be used by the programmers as these words are reserved by

VBA. If any of these words arise in your code, you will get a compile error.

* * *

Getting Familiarize with the VBA Data Types

When I say the word data type, I am mainly referring to a way in which the program written in VBA stores data in memory. VBA gives us the leverage to not to assign a data type to every variable, but if you leave it on VBA there's definitely some cost to it. The automatic assignment of data types may result in slower execution and wastage of memory. Applications that are small in size may not be affected by the automatic declaration, but the large and complex application does have an impact on them. It's always a good practice to declare the data type of the variables that you are going to use. Although the list is long, below are the most common types of data that VBA can handle.

Data type	Bytes Used	Range of Values
Byte	1	0 to 255
Boolean	2	True or False
Integer	2	-32768 to 32768
Long	4	-2,147,483,648 to 2,147,483,648
Double	8	-1.79E308 to -4.94E-324 for negative values
Currency	8	-922,337,203,685,477 to 922,337,203,685,477
Date	8	1/1/0100 to 12/31/9999
String	1 per char	Varies
Variant	Varies	Varies

A good rule of thumb is to use the variable with the smallest size but it should also serve your purpose.

* * *

Declaring Variables and their scope

By now, I am sure you must be familiarized with about variables and their data types. In this section, we will now be declaring a variable to a data type.if a variable is not declared in your macros, the VBA itself will define it to default data type: Variant. For example, if a particular variable is by default set to be a variant, and it contains a text string that looks like a number (eg 123), this variable, however, can be used for both the numeric and string calculations. As mentioned earlier, it is always a good practice to declare the data type of your variable else the VBA tool will assign the data type as variant and the variant results in time-consuming checks and this ultimately uses memory. One good way to force yourself to declare the data types of the variables is to write the following statement as the first statement in your VBA module:

```
Option Explicit
```

This statement forces you to declare all data types of your variables, as it will throw a compile error if any variable is left undeclared.

A variable is using declared by using the Dim statement.

Let's look at some examples:

```
Dim Employee_name As String
Dim Employee_Salary As Long
Dim X
Dim Amount As Double
```

All the variables in the above example have been defined a particular data type apart from the variable "X". The variable X will, however, be treated as a variable.

Apart from Dim, to declare variables we can use three other keywords:

✓ Private
✓ Static
✓ Public

Let's look at an example to get a good picture of the declarations of the data type of variables.

```
Sub Variables()
Dim Name As String
Name = "Anum Haroon"

Dim Age As Integer
Age = 21

Dim Birthdate As Date
Birthdate = 19 / 11 / 1991

MsgBox "Name is " & Name & Chr(10) & "Age is " & Age & " And Birthdate is " & Birthdate

End Sub
```

When the above VBA code is executed, a message
is prompted on the screen. The message box is as
follows:

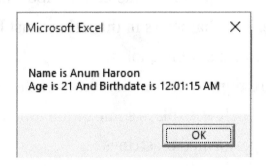

Chapter 2:

Strings

Playing with characters

Now let's have fun by playing with the strings
in the VBA tool. Strings fundamentally
compromise of characters that are arranged in a
sequence. The characters in the string can consist
of alphabets, special characters, numbers or any
of these. The characters in the string must be
enclosed with double quotes.

There are numerous functionalities of the string.
The table below displays some of the functions
that are performed on strings.

Function name	Returns
Str()	*A string representation of a number*
Val()	*A numerical*

	representation of a number
Trim()	*To remove spaces in a string*
Left()	*To get a portion of the string from the left side*
Right()	*To extract a portion from the right side*
Mid()	*To extract any part of the string*
Len()	*To retrieve the number of characters in the string*
StrCov()	*To convert the string to some other format*
UCase()	*Convert all characters to uppercase*
LCase()	*Convert all characters to lower case*

The Excel VBA handles two types of strings:

✓ Fixed-Length Strings
✓ Variable-Length Strings

As far as the fixed-length strings are concerned, they mainly contain a fixed number of characters. The maximum number of characters they can store is 65,526. The second type of string is the Variable-Length String. The variable-length string can store a massive number of characters. Whenever you declare a string, it's always a good practice to declare the maximum length of the string otherwise the VBA tool will handle it on its own. Below is an example of declaring a fixed length string.

```
Dim MyName As String * 20
```

Let's write a macro code and play with some functionalities of the string. I would like to call the procedure as "Play_With_Strings".

```
Sub Play_With_Strings()

Dim Name As String
Dim FirstName As String
Dim LastName As String
Dim SpaceLoc As Integer

Name = "Anum Haroon"

SpaceLoc = InStr(1, Name, " ")

FirstName = Left(Name, SpaceLoc - 1)

LastName = Mid(Name, SpaceLoc + 1, Len(Name) - SpaceLoc)

MsgBox (" The full name is " & Name & ", the first name is " & FirstName & " and the last name is " & LastName)

End Sub
```

Now let's decode it step-by-step. The first four
statements in the procedure are the part where
the variables are declared. All the first three
variables have been set as strings and the last one
has been declared as an integer. Now after the
variable declaration section, we begin by
assigning values to the variables. I first stored a
name in the Name variable. Now next I wanted to
find out the location of the space between my first
name and the last name. Space is located through
the InStr() function. The InStr() has three input
parameters. The first parameters decide from
where position should the function start

searching in the string. The second parameter is the string that needs to be traversed,and finally, the third parameter defines what needs to be searched. In this example, in the variable value "Anum Haroon", we want to search the location of the space. Once this is found out, the value is stored in SpaceLoc variable. Now we want to retrieve the first and last name and then store in the variables respectively. To do this we will be using the Left() and Mid() function of the string. The Left() function has two inputs. The first input is the string whereas the second input defines the position till where the string needs to be extracted. So by passing the SpaceLoc and the Name variable we can get the first name. To get the last name, we will be using the Mid() function. The Mid() Function has three inputs that are the string, the start, and the end position. We will be passing the name variable, the SpaceLoc position and then the end position which is basically equal to the string length. The last statement is written in the VBA Code to generate an output on the screen. We will again be binding the VBA code to a button. Once the button is executed, the following values will pop up on the screen.

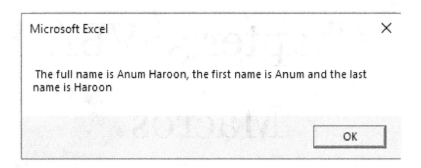

Not too bad prospective Programmers! You now must be having a good understanding of how you can play with the string functions. String function can be convenient especially when you have to manipulate large datasets. Instead of retrieving all the functionality manually you can write a macro code, bind it with a button and you're good to go.

Chapter 3: VBA Macros

Jumping to an advanced level

So far, we have covered some basics of the VBA Macros. We will now be pacing up our game by jumping over to an advanced level. VBA Macros has considerably made the lives of excel users easy. With the implementation of VBA Macros in your worksheet, you can significantly save up time by automating your operations of excel. Instead of working on large data sets manually, formatting thousands of records, applying formulas to manipulate data, you can write a VBA Macro, bind it with the excel sheet and do all the operations within seconds.

In the section, we will be working on some examples of VBA Macros. This section will compromise of the following subtopics:

- ✓ Worksheet Ranges
- ✓ Exploring some Excel Settings
- ✓ Pacing up your VBA Code

* * *

Worksheet Ranges

The VBA programming has got a lot to do with the ranges on the worksheet. The following points need to be kept in mind whenever we are working with range objects:

- ✓ If you are not associating the worksheet name to the range in your code, then you must ensure that the sheet on which you want your macros to run must be in the active state

- ✓ Excel gives the users the ability to select multiple ranges

- ✓ The Macro recorder doesn't always create the best code. You can always edit the Macro generated code to make it more efficient

One of the most frequently used operations of the Excel Macros is copying a range. If you are using the macro recorder to generate you a code while copying a range, you will get the below code.

```
Sub Range ()

  Range ("A1:A5") .Select

  Selection.Copy

  Range ("B1") .Select

  ActiveSheet.Paste

  Application.CutCopyMode = False

End Sub
```

One other operation of the range function is the Selection ability. We often want to select a block of cells and then do some operations on it. Instead of giving reference to each cell, we can collectively refer the entire block of cells in one statement. Please find below an example of the

Selection operation on the range statement.

```
Sub Select_Range_Down()
  Range(ActiveCell, ActiveCell.End(xlDown)).Select
End Sub
```

In the above code, the VBA procedure is beginning to select the cells from the active cell. It is then extending the range until a blank cell arises.

```
Sub Select_Range_Down()
  Range(ActiveCell, ActiveCell.End(xlDown)).Select
End Sub
```

One other exciting feature of VBA Macros is the selection of the entire column or the entire row. The following is an example of the selection of the entire row.

```
Sub SelectRow()

 ActiveCell.EntireRow.Select

End Sub
```

Similarly, the entire column functionality of excel
can also be used to select the entire column.

* * *

Exploring some Excel Settings

The operation of some procedures in Excel
Macros can be changed by one or more Excel's
settings. One interesting setting is the Boolean
setting. In this setting, you give a False or a True
value to the excel procedure and then the setting
is altered accordingly. Let's look at an example. In
Excel Macros, you can give page breaks on your
worksheet. You can turn on the Page break
feature of excel by passing a real value to the
DisplayPageBreaks procedure.

```
ActiveSheet.DisplayPageBreaks = True
```

Similarly, we can turn off this feature by passing a false value.

```
ActiveSheet.DisplayPageBreaks = False
```

* * *

Pacing up your VBA Code

VBA is a first way to perform data manipulations on your worksheet. In this section, we will be discussing some useful tips to further optimize the VBA Code to pace your operations.

One feature of excel is that whenever you execute the Excel Macros, the updates are visible on the screen. This, however, can have an impact on the performance of your code. You can, however, disable the setting. To do this, write down the below code.

```
Application.ScreenUpdating = False
```

This will turn off the screen updates while the

Macros is being executed. To turn on the feature again, execute the below code.

```
Application.ScreenUpdating = True
```

One other way to speed up your Macros is by disabling the automatic calculation feature. If there are a lot of complicated formulas on your worksheet, by setting the calculation mode to the manual can significantly speed up things in your code. Execute the below statement to make the calculation manual.

```
Application.Calculation = xlCalculationManual
```

Macros display alerts messages to the users while the code is being executed. In this case, if the Excel is unattended and the Macros is executing then the alert message will bring the code to a halt. They require the humans to respond to the alert messages. However, there is an option to disable the alert messages so that the Macros is not brought to a halt.

```
Application.DisplayAlerts = False
```

You can also turn the alerts by writing a
statement at the end of your code. To do this, we
will just change the DisplayAlerts statements to a
True condition.

```
Application.DisplayAlerts = True
```

Another to pace up the speed of your Macro
Program is to ensure that you declare variables at
the start of your code. It is imperative that you
declare the data type of all the variables. Although
Excel doesn't throw an error if a variable's data
type is left undefined but Excel won't know the
exact size of the variable. As a result of this, Excel
might assign space much more extensive than
what it is required. This will result in extra
memory consumption and can also decrease the
performance of your code.

Chapter 4: Loops

Repeating blocks of VBA

Loops are essential as they make macros more capable and they also make the code easier to write. Instead of writing numerous statements for every cell on the worksheet, loops help to simplify your code. Several types of loops are supported in VBA.

For-Next loop in the programming language is referred to as the simplest type of loop. There is a control variable that acts as a counter to the loop condition. The counter begins from the start value and continues to be executed till the end value is reached. Code that is written between the For statement and the next statement is repeated in the loop. Let's look at an example.

```
Sub Multiply()

  Dim Product As Double

  Dim Counter As Integer

  Product = 0

  For Counter = 1 To 50

  Product = Product * Counter

  Next Counter

  MsgBox Product

End Sub
```

In the above example, we are performing a
multiplication operation in the For-Next Loop.
The counter will begin from 1 and continue to
execute till the counter value is reached 50. There
is the only statement written in the For-Next loop.
The statement multiplies the counter value with
the Product value and stores it in the Product
variable. When the For-Next loop counter value is
reached till 50, the Product value will be
displayed on the screen. However, it is not
advisable to change the counter value in the For-
Next Statement as it can generate unpredictable
results. For-Next loop can also include Exit

statement within the block. The Exit statements are placed in the For-Next block to terminate the loop immediately.

In the following example, an Exit Statement has been inserted in the For-Next loop.

```
Sub Exit_Statement()

    Dim a As Integer

    a = 10

    For i = 0 To a

        MsgBox ("The value is i is : " & i)

        If i = 4 Then

            i = i * 10

            MsgBox ("The value is i is : " & i)

            Exit For

        End If

    Next

End Sub
```

The MsgBox will display the value of i. The value of i is incremented. As shown in the above example, when the value of I will be equal to 4, the code will enter in the if statement. In the if statement, the value of i is first multiplied by 10 and then it will be printed on the screen. Soon after this, an exit statement will be executed which will end the loop immediately. When the above code is executed, the following output will be displayed on the screen sequentially.

```
The value is i is : 0

The value is i is : 1

The value is i is : 2

The value is i is : 3

The value is i is : 40
```

The exit statements can be beneficial especially when we want to handle exceptions or errors in our code. If for example, there is a chance that a garbage value can come in a specific variable. I don't handle the garbage value, there is a chance that loop will be executed till infinity. This can result in memory overload. To cater to this scenario, the exit statements are placed so that the loop is terminated immediately.

Another type of loop is the Nested For-Next loop. The nested statement comes in handy when you want to loop through tabular data or multidimensional data. A table has data placed in both columns and rows. One loop is used to traverse through the columns whereas the other loop can be used to traverse through the rows. This is how you use the nested For-Next loop.In the following example, we will be filling up data in both the rows and the columns.

```
Sub Fill_Table()

  Dim Col As Long

  Dim Row As Long

  Dim i As Integer

  i = 0

  For Col = 1 To 3

    For Row = 1 To 3

      i = i + 1

      Cells(Row, Col) = i

    Next Row

  Next Col

End Sub
```

In this example, we will be filling up a 3 columns x 3 rows table. The outer for loop fills up the data in the columns whereas the inner for loop fills up the data in the rows. The output of the code can be seen below.

◢	A	B	C
1	1	4	7
2	2	5	8
3	3	6	9
4			

Another type of looping structure which is
supported the VBA is the Do-While loop. The
statements in the Do-While will keep on
executing repeatedly until the mentioned
conditioned is fulfilled.

```
Sub DoWhileDemo()

  Do While ActiveCell.Value <> Empty

  ActiveCell.Value = ActiveCell.Value * 2

  ActiveCell.Offset(1, 0).Select

  Loop

End Sub
```

In the above example, a Do-While loop is
inserted. The Do statement checks whether the
active cell is empty or not. If the cell is not empty,
the active cell is multiplied by and then the next
cell is select. Whenever the code will encounter an
empty cell, the do-while loop will break. One

should always ensure that there should be some break statement in the loop else the loop will keep on executing till infinity. This, however, can result in memory overflow. Loops considerably save up the space of the code and make it look compact and less complicated. However, loop statements do not reduce the time the code takes to execute.

Chapter 5: Arrays

Storing collection of elements

Arrays are usually supported by all programming languages. Arrays are also supported by VBA thus making life easier for programmers. An array is used where we want to collect data of similar type into one single variable. In an array, data is stored in a sequential manner. Each element in the array is provided an index number. The index number can be stated as a reference to the elements stored in the array. For example, we can define an array to store the names of the days of the week. If the array is named as Weekdays, the first element in the array will be stated as Weekdays(1). Similarly, the second element will be stated as Weekdays(2), the third as Weekdays(3) and so on.In order to use the array, it is mandatory to first declare the data type of array. VBA does not give us the flexibility to leave an array undeclared. Just like other regular variables, an array can be declared by either using a Dim statement or a Public statement. However, one additional thing about the array is that you need to mention the number of elements the array will hold. The syntax for declaring an array can be seen below.

```
Dim Dec_Array(0 To 10) As Integer
```

You declare the first index number, the keyword To and then finally the last index number. All this is enclosed inside the parentheses. One flexibility VBA offers is that you don't necessarily have to mention the lower index every time. In this case, VBA assumes that the lower index is 0. For example, the above statement can also be written as:

```
Dim Dec_Array(10) As Integer
```

VBA by default assumes the lower index to be zero. However, if you don't want VBA to assume the lower index to zero, you can use the Option Base statement to force VBA to change the lower index accordingly. For example, if you want VBA to assume the lower index to be always set to 1 then you should write:

```
Option Base 1
```

You also need to ensure that this statement is written before the declaration of the array.

So far, we have discussed one-dimensional arrays. A more natural explanation of the one-dimensional array is a single line of a value of the same data type. When we want to have more than one dimension in an array, this is known as the multi-dimensional array. VBA can handle up to 60 dimensions in the multi-dimensional array. However, this is a sporadic case in which 60 dimensions are being used in the VBA code. A multidimensional array is also declared using the Dim statement.

```
Dim Multi_Dim(1 To 10, 1 To 100) As String
```

This is a multi-dimensional array. The first index of the multi-dimensional array ranges from 1 to 10, whereas the range for the second index is from 1 to 100. This results in the declaration of 1000 elements in the array. The numbers are stored in a tabular arrangement of 10 rows x 100 columns. To refer any element in the array, you have to mention two index number. The first index number will be the row and the second index number will be the column. For example, if we want to assign a value to the element in the 2nd row and 4th column, we will write it as:

```
Multi_Dim(2, 4) = 10
```
The value 10 will be stored in the element of the array that is placed in the 2nd row and 4th column. Dynamic arrays are also supported by VBA. The advantage about using a dynamic array is that you don't have to declare the number of elements it will hold at the start of your code. The array size is declared at runtime. Dynamic arrays help to save

Chapter 6: Functions

Performing Specific Tasks

L et's first define what exactly is a function. A function can be called a procedure that performs some sort of calculation. A function returns a single value. Let's take an example, the Sum function will return the sum of the values that it will intake. Similarly, in VBA macros the function undergoes a specific calculation and then finally return a single value.

The function that you utilize in your VBA code primarily comes from three areas:

✓ Worksheet functions
✓ Some Built-in functions
✓ Customize functions that are defined according to your needs

Playing with built-in functions

Well the good thing about using VBA is that it has made the life of programmer easy by defining some built-in Functions. You don't have to write every function from the scratch. You just need to know the exact name of the function and Voila! Let's look at some built-in functions of the VBA tool.

```
Sub DisplayDate()

MsgBox "The Date is: " & Date

End Sub
```

The above procedure has been created to display the system date. In this scenario, we have used the built-in excel function, Date. The Date function doesn't require any input arguments. We can also retrieve the time by writing Time instead of Date. Time again is also a built-in function of the   excel   tool.
Let's look at another example

```
Sub Get_String_Length()

Dim Name As String
Dim StringLength As Integer

Name = "Anum Haroon"
StringLength = Len(Name)

MsgBox Name & " has " & StringLength & " characters"


End Sub
```

In the above example, we wanted to retrieve the string length of the name. We, therefore, used the excel built-in function, Len().

If we want to retrieve the year or the month from the system date.

```
Sub Display_Month()

Dim Month_Name As Long

Month_Name = Month(Date)

MsgBox MonthName(Month_Name)


End Sub
```

In the above procedure, we are basically using the Built-in Month function to retrieve the Month from the System Date. Further, we are also using the MonthName Function in order to display the month name.

There are specific functions in the VBA tool that come up with some additional functionalities. For example, the MsgBox is a convenient function. Every time a user uses the MsgBox function in its Macros, a screen is popped up at whatever line it is executed. This MsgBox can be very handy to prompt the user about the values that are stored in the variables. Moreover, it also helps to debug the code and find out any potential errors in the code. There is another convenient function which is known as the InputBox function. The InputBox function gives the user the capability to enter a value into a simple box that is displayed. The value that is retrieved through the InputBox can be further manipulated in the macros that we have written.

The VBA tool facilitates the user with lots of built-in functionality. The question is that how do you locate those functions? Well, that's not an issue at all. You can retrieve a list of all the built-in function by typing VBA followed by a period as shown in the diagram below

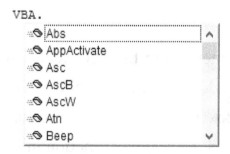

In order to find out the details linked to a particular function, enter the name of the function in the VBA module, move the pointer on the text and then press F1. You will be prompted with a new window screen and help wizard will open up.

Although the list of inbuilt functions is exceptionally long, I have compiled some important ones in the table below.

* * *

Exploring the worksheet functions

One other interesting feature of the Excel VBA is the worksheet functions. A worksheet is an area where the cells are placed and the data is manipulated on the cells. In a nutshell, the worksheet is the workspace where basically all the calculations and the manipulations take place. When we are accessing functions using the "WorksheetFunction" expression, the manipulation or calculation is performed on the active sheet. By active sheet, I basically mean the sheet that is currently open on the screen.

Let's look at an example of a worksheet's sum function.

```
Total_Amount = Application.WorksheetFunction.Sum(Range("B1:B3"))
```

In the above example, "Total_Amount" is the variable in which the sum of the cells is being stored. Range("B1: B3") refers to the cells on the worksheet of which the sum has to be taken. VBA also gives the user's to access the Sum function directly either from the Application part of the WorksheetFunction part. VBA has the ability to figure out what exactly you are performing. Smart Right? The following three statements have exactly the same output.

```
Total_Amount = Application.WorksheetFunction.Sum(Range("B1:B3"))

Total_Amount = WorksheetFunction.Sum(Range("B1:B3"))

Total_Amount = Application.Sum(Range("B1:B3"))
```

I personally prefer to perform my calculations using the WorksheetFunction to have a better understanding of the code that is executing. Let's look at some more Worksheet Functions.

To calculate the Min Value in a range

```
Sub Find_Min()

Dim MinNum As Double

MinNum = WorksheetFunction.Min(Range("B1:B10"))

MsgBox ("The Minimum Value is " & MinNum)

End Sub
```

In the above example, the Minimum value is calculated from the range of cells from B1 till B10. The value is stored in the variable MinNum. The output of the above expression can be seen in the diagram below

B	C	D	E	F	G	H	I
10							
11							
15							
20							
3							
7					Microsoft Excel	✕	cula
19							
14					The Minimum Value is 3		
16							
20					OK		

Similarly, you can also calculate the maximum value from the Range using the Max() function of the worksheet.

Vlookup Function

If you have ever interacted with an excel programmer, I am sure you must have heard about the Vlookup Function. You can never be an Excel Guru if you don't know how to implement the Vlookup Function. Vlookup is a potent function as it can help you the exact information from a table of any size. The Vlookup Function intakes four parameters. The first parameter represents the item that needs to be searched in the table. For example, in the below example we are looking for the product B. The second Parameters represents the range in which it needs to be looked up, the third parameter represents the column number that we want to return as a result, and finally, the four parameter intakes a true or a false value. The true value tells the vlookup to return a value that can be an approximate match whereas the false value tells the vlookup to only return a value when there is an exact match. In the following example, the user will be entering the product name in order to retrieve its price from the table. The product name will be entered using the InputBox Function. The price of the product will then be displayed on the output screen using the MsgBox Function.

```
Sub Get_Product_Price()

Dim Product

Dim Price As Integer

Product = InputBox("Enter the Product ")

Price = WorksheetFunction.VLookup(Product, Range("A2:B5"), 2, 0)

MsgBox ("The Product Price of " & Product & " is " & Price)

End Sub
```

As shown in the below diagram, the input box is prompted on the screen when the Macros is executed.

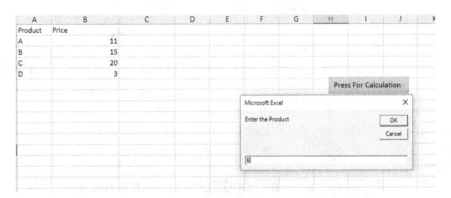

In the example, the Product B was Entered. On pressing the Ok button, the Output was displayed.

The Input was passed to the Vlookup Function. The Vlookup Function traversed on the Product B and returned the Price of the Product.

Conclusion

And We are almost done!

By the end of this chapter, you must have become very much familiar with the Excel VBA. In this section, I will just briefly gives some essential guidelines.

It is always a good practice to declare your variables at the start of your code. Leaving your variables undefined will only save you from few seconds but later on, you will have to bear with the consequences. So make a habit to declare all the variables at the start. This will significantly impact on your code quality.

Once you are done finalizing your code and everything is running perfecting, make sure you do the last minute clean up of your code. Make sure all the code lines are indented. This will help you understand your code better when you will review it later. Make sure all your variables are declared and the description of the variable should be relevant to their actual operation. For example, if a variable will be holding Amount in it so a good practice it is to name it as "Amount" rather than naming it as XYZ. It is always a good practice to add comments in your code. Do a quick check to remove any redundancy in your code.

As Macros can compromise multiple procedures, therefore you shouldn't avoid putting all the calculations in one procedure. For example, the procedure for calculating Sum should be in a separate procedure. The procedure for converting string values to date value should be in a separate procedure and so on.

One last advice is to make sure that you take a backup of your code every now and then. It takes an effort to make a correct macro code and there is always a chance that your Excel Workbook can get corrupted. So to save yourself from all the re-work, make sure to take a backup after every few days.

Welcome to the last page reader, I'm happy to see you here I hope you had a great time reading my book and if you want to support my work you are welcome to share your thoughts and leave a review.

Respectfully,
William B. Skates